T0163507

A Bit of Air

EMERGING VOICES FROM THE MIDDLE EAST

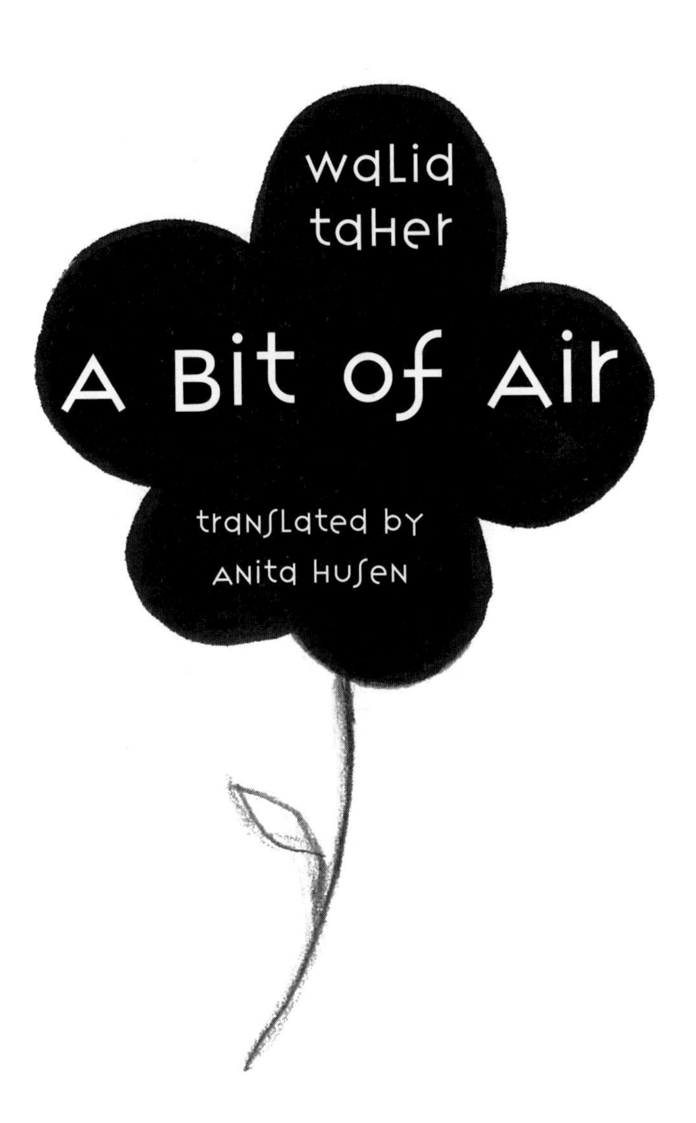

The Center for Middle Eastern Studies

The University of Texas at Austin

Printed in the United States of America

Translator: Anita Husen
Cover art: © Walid Taher
Cover and text design: Kristi Shuey
Editor: Wendy E. Moore

Library of Congress Control Number: 2012950843
ISBN: 978-0-292-74238-3

Habbet Hawa
by Walid Taher

introduction

Originally published in Egypt in 2008, *A Bit of Air* (*Habbet Hawa*) proved a surprise hit for author and illustrator Walid Taher (b. Cairo, Egypt, 1969)—perhaps in large part because it so accurately portrayed the sense of discontent in the country that would boil over in the uprising of January 2011. More like a toy or puzzle than a traditional book, its weave of drawings, doodles, anecdotes, and aphorisms wraps the reader up in the complexity of the human experience. This English translation preserves the Arabic text that is so integral to the illustrations while introducing a new audience to Walid Taher's world of dark humor.

Since early in his career, Taher has enjoyed popularity as a children's author, garnering national, regional, and international awards for such titles as *The Black Dot* and *Animal Dreams*. He has also published a series of colorfully illustrated books that follow the adventures of a precocious and irreverent boy named Fizo. The vivid colors and playful dialogue of the *Fizo* series appeal to children's sense of fantasy and adventure, while the humor draws in both children and their parents.

A Bit of Air is Taher's first book to push beyond his usual genre of children's literature. When first published, it was an unexpected hit across generations in Egypt and throughout the Arabic-speaking world. It has received abundant critical acclaim in major newspapers and in blogs on Arabic literature. The book's large fan base comes from many different sectors of society: from religious to secular, bourgeois to working-class, activist to apathetic, and educated to semi-literate.

This broad appeal comes from the book's novelty on the one hand, and its uncanny familiarity on the other. *A Bit of Air* blends images and text in an avant-garde approach to literary writing, reflecting the emergence of comics and cartoons as cutting-edge contemporary genres. In short, it represents the integration of a new genre into the mainstream of contemporary Arabic literature. Though the increase in readership of graphic novels certainly has contributed to the popularity of this book, *A Bit of Air* is not itself a conventional graphic novel. Rather, its uniqueness lies in its approach to the graphic form. Instead of following one story line or focusing on one character, *A Bit of Air* tackles many different themes in a seemingly random arrangement, making it almost impossible to trace the author's thought process from one page to the next. Each stand-alone page presents a profound yet simple observation, many of which have become mantras for Taher's readers; thus it is better viewed as a collection of independent vignettes. Such an approach leaves room for readers to see reflections of themselves in the text. If one page does not resonate, the page before or after likely will.

The text and images of *A Bit of Air* also exemplify the mood of the Egyptian people just prior to the revolutions that rocked the Arab world beginning in 2011. One can find hints of the frustration and fatalism that Egyptians felt about the economic stagnation and political gridlock gripping their country. An example of this is the illustration on page 104 of a man standing alone and sad, head tilted to one side and looking down, dressed in tattered clothing and holding a small flag. The accompanying text reads:

> **To you I pledge my love**
> My poverty, my misery, and my debt
> My failures and frustration with my meager salary
> To you I pledge my humiliation,
> My head hung low
> And my eyes avoiding those of my children
> For whom I can't provide
> **To you I pledge my heart!**

The first and last lines are taken from the Egyptian national anthem. Taher updates this notion of patriotism by remixing the national anthem to reflect the frustrated state of Egyptian society.

Though the themes capture a pre-revolutionary ethos in their focus and inspiration, they also poignantly encompass Egypt's post-revolutionary era as well. From the start of the January 25, 2011, uprising that led to the ouster of longtime president Hosni Mubarak, Taher has published a cartoon each day in *Shorouk News*, one of Egypt's largest independent dailies. Taher and his images, both those in *Shorouk News* and *A Bit of Air*, have since become icons of the Egyptian revolution. For example, a now-famous panel (pages 70 and 71) from *A Bit of Air* that depicts a man urinating against a wall uses potty humor as a general critique of the fortification of borders and splintering of urban space. Thanks to an award-winning song, "The Wall," by Egyptian singer Youssra El-Hawary, the image and its text now specifically represent the wall separating Tahrir Square, the epicenter of the revolution, from the nearby Ministry of the Interior.

This translation seeks to preserve the rhythm of the original Arabic through linguistic and cultural specificity. *A Bit of Air* mostly employs colloquial Egyptian Arabic, which is captured in translation through the use of conversational English, including unconventional grammar, contractions, hanging prepositions, and a generally earthy lexicon. Where the register of Arabic elevates to the more formal Modern Standard Arabic, the translation reflects this shift with more formal English.

Since this edition is bilingual, the translation mimics the graphic arrangement of the Arabic text. Specifically, it mimics the original punctuation, layout, and formatting so readers can easily toggle between the two texts. The images on each page and, more precisely, the effect of the interplay between image and text helped to guide the translation. For example, on page 48 there is a man standing indoors, looking out a window; the literal "in front of the glass" is translated to "outside my window," as suggested by the image.

In instances where strict translation does not capture the cultural connotation of a word or phrase, a parallel English idiom is used. Colloquialisms were selected for their ability to convey the original message while at the same time allowing for sound repetition and phonetic resonance. An example of this is the use of the phrase "an average Joe" for "*wahid ᶜadi*" instead of the literal translation, "average one," in order to allow for a reflection of the rhyme in the original Arabic: "*ᶜadi/hadi/ᶜadi*" to "Joe/slow/Joe."

The pun in the title, however, cannot be fully captured in English translation. *Hawa* can mean both "air" and "passion." While the passage (page 23) from which the title was taken implies the first meaning, the latter is subtly present in the different sentiments on each page, which vacillate between political and emotional, satirical and desperate, sweet and sarcastic.

This publication would not have been possible without the help of many. I owe deep gratitude to my Arabic instructors, and to all my teachers since kindergarten, who have inspired me to learn and teach. I am indebted to my friends in Egypt who showed me the richness of their language and culture, particularly to Fadi Awad, who gave me this book, and to Walid Taher himself, for his encouragement and cooperation. This book would not exist without Tarek El-Ariss and Wendy Moore, whose idea it was to turn the translation into a bilingual edition, and whose enthusiasm and efforts led to this publication. Any mistakes are my responsibility.

Anita Husen

Translator

A Bit of Air

• بسسسس! ......

* أنا؟

• Pssst! ......

* Me?

جوّايا حد زَعْلان

من إني ...

زعلان من حد جوّايا !

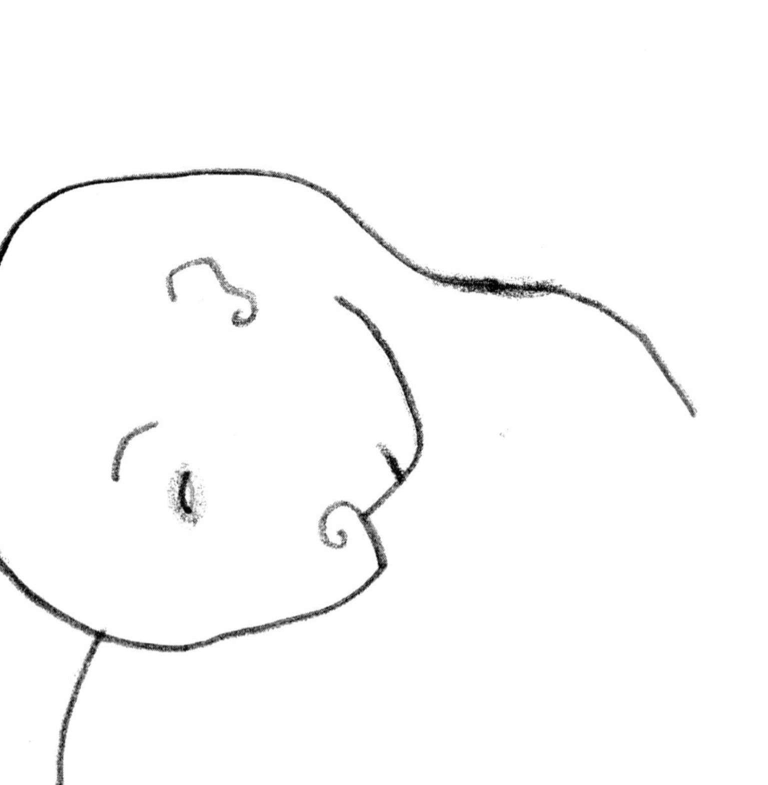

Someone deep inside me is sad

That I am . . .

Sad with someone deep inside me!

كُل شئ كان عادى . . .
و المقابلة كانت عاديّة
عدّى الوقت . .
واكتشفت . . .
إن كل اللّحظات هَيبقى
لحظات تاريخيّة !

Everything was ordinary . . .

The meeting was ordinary

With the passing of time . .

I came to find . . .

Everything that happened would become

History in the making!

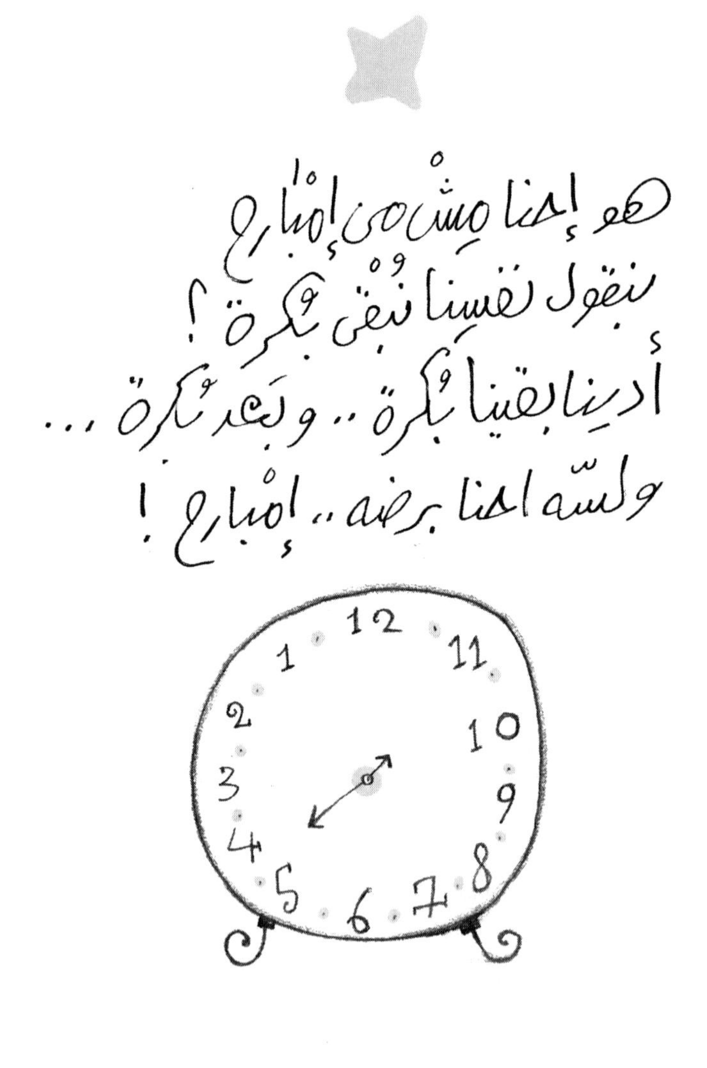
هو إحنا مش من إمبارح
بنقول نفسنا نبقى بكرة ؟
أدينا بقينا بكرة .. وبعد بكرة ...
ولسه إحنا برضه .. إمبارح !

Haven't we been telling ourselves since yesterday

That we wish tomorrow would come?

Now tomorrow is upon us . . and the day after . . .

While we're still stuck . . in yesterday!

أوضة ساكتة
فيها مجنون ساكت
عَمّال يحاول من سنة
إنّه يفضل مُتّزن
فى الوضْع الثابت !!

A silent room

In it a silent madman

Who's been trying for a year

To remain balanced

In a fixed position!!

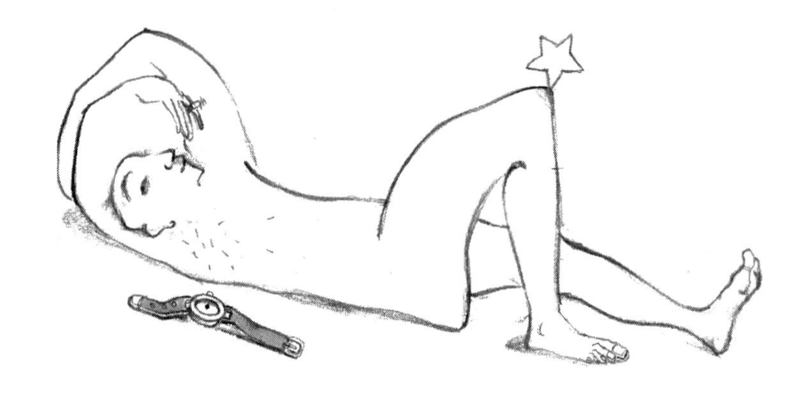

قلعت (النهاردة)
ودخلت أنام
ماجاليش نوم
خايف بكره مايجيش
وأعيش عريان... من غير يوم!

I stripped down (today)

And went to bed

Sleep didn't come

For fear tomorrow wouldn't come

And I live on naked . . . . . without another day!

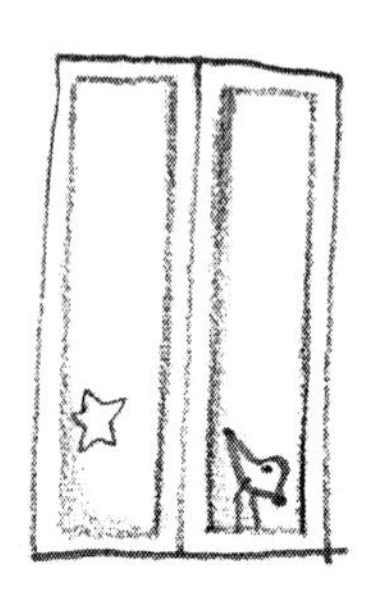

فيه ناس دايماً واحشاني
معرفش مين هُمَّه ...!

There are people I'm missing all the time

I just don't know who they are . . !

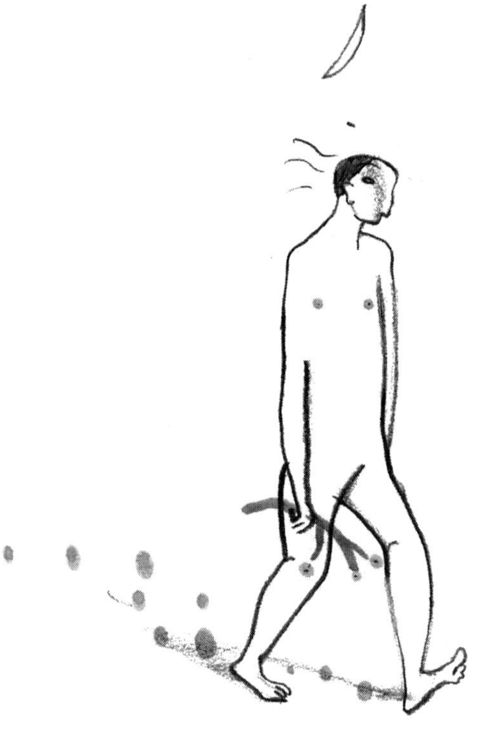

سيبوني حُرّ طَفْشان عَرْيان....
قالوالى .. لأ .. كده تِعْيا ..
قلت .. يعنى أنا كده ...... مِشْ عَيّان ؟!

Leave me to wander around free, naked . . . .

They said: "Don't, you'll catch a cold."

I replied: "As if I'm not sick already?!"

نعيش زي الفلاسفه تعساء
ونحاول نفهم الفوله
واللا خلينا كده
بلهاء .. سعداء
بالدنيا المجهولة ؟!

Should we live like philosophers in misery
Trying to turn over each stone
Or remain as we are
Fools . . happy
With the world unknown?

قرقضت كل ضوافري
متوتر... متشعفرط
الحياه عمّاله تتركب.. تتعقد
وأنا كنت فاكرها
هتبقى... أبسط...!

My nails are all chewed up

I am worked up . . . fed up

Life's complications are piling up

I used to think

Things would eventually . . . let up . . !

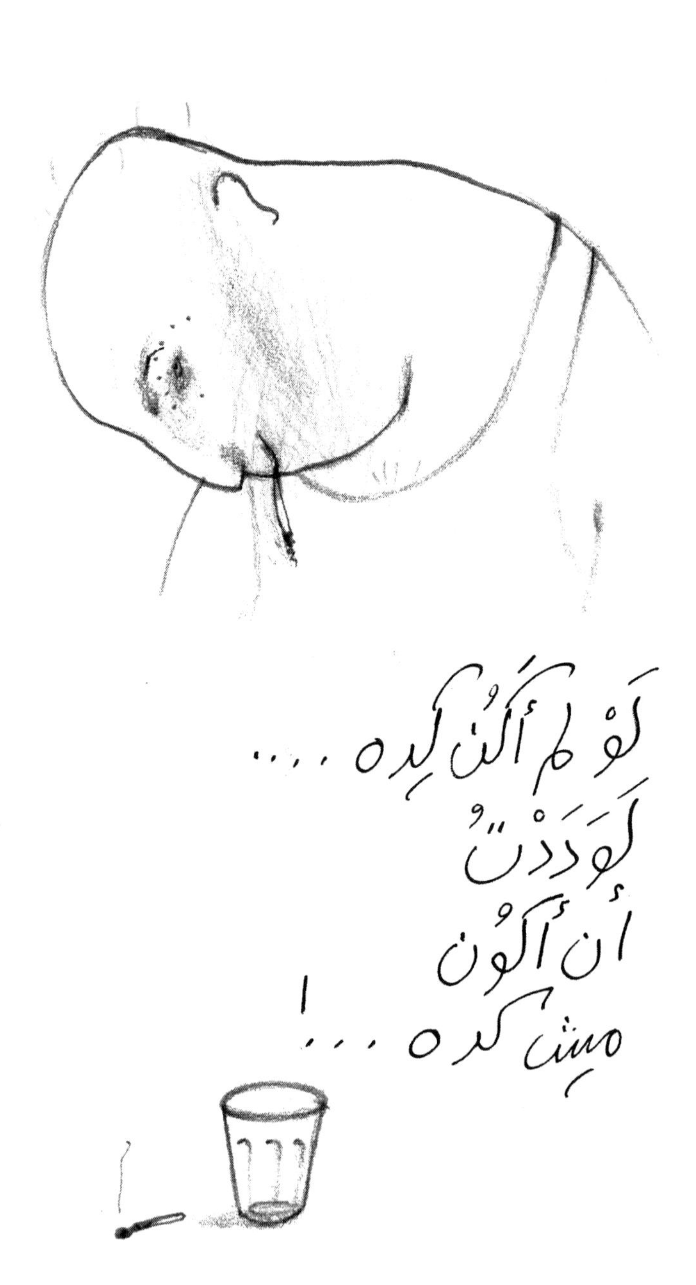
لو لم أكن كده ....
لوددتُ
أن أكون
مش كده ...!

Were I not this way . . . .

I would have wished

Not to be

This way . . ![*]

[*]Play on the famous saying by Egyptian nationalist Mustafa Kamil: "Were I not Egyptian, I would have wished to be Egyptian."

حبّة هوا
طيّروا الورق كُلّه
ياللا مش مهم
هوّ ايه اللى كان فى الورق
أحلى من الهوا ؟!

A bit of air

Blowing away all the papers

Whatever, why care

What on those papers

Could be better than air?!

ماشى ع البحر صافى
مدلدل كتافى
الميه ساقعه والرمل دافى
أى ...
دخل فى رجلى سؤال
آدى آخرة
اللى تمشى حافى !

A long walk on the beach

With my shoulders slumped

Taking in the cool water, warm sand

Ouch . . .

I stepped on a sharp question

That's what you get

For walking barefoot!

.... غرقانين ..؟!

وإيه يعني نفضل غرقانين ....

حتى فرصة نعيش مع السمك ... هاديين ..

بلا مشاكل .....

بلا خناقات ...

بلا كواخة بني آدمين !

. . . . Drowning . . ?!

So what if we continue to drown . . .

It's a chance to live among the fish . . . tranquil . .

Without problems . . . . .

Without bickering . . .

Without the pettiness of humans!

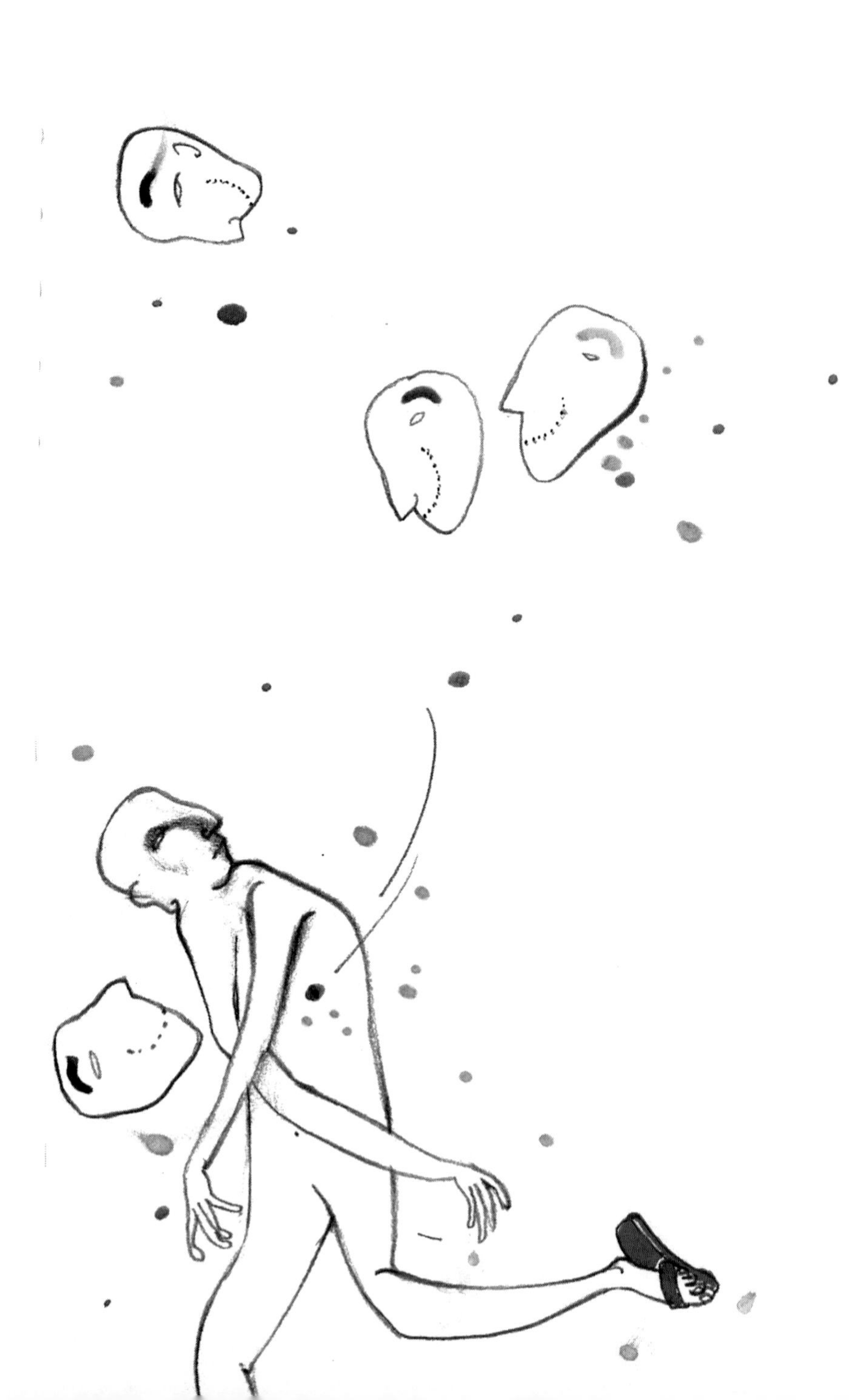

عفاريت عريانه بتطير حواليه
مش خايفة مني ... مع إني
عمال أهشهم بإيديه
بعصبية . . . .
وكل ما يبعدوا .. يرجعوا تاني
عشان ...
يضحكوا عليه !

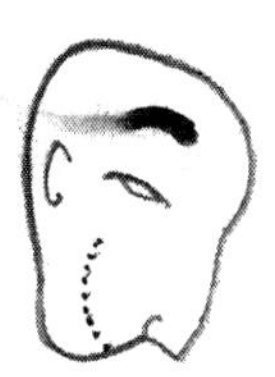

Naked spirits fly around me

Fearlessly . . . even though

I keep shooing them away

Anxiously . . . . .

Each time they go away, they come back again

Only to . . .

Make fun of me!

يا ملاك .. انت عندك جناحين
وُأنا عندى ... إيدين
إنْت تعْرف تُطير
أمّا أنا
هأعرف منين !

Oh angel . . you have two wings

While I have . . . two arms

You can fly

As for me

How can I!

They are both a bit loony

Poor things . . .

I don't know which made the other this way

She used to tell him:

Even the grossest person in Egypt

Brushes his teeth

While your cabinet

Is full of toothpaste!

الإثنين مجانين

مساكين ...

ما أعرفش مين جنّن مين

كانت تقول له :

أوحش واحد في مصر

يغسل سنانه

مع إن دولابك

مليان معاجين !

أنا شربت القهوة على مزاجي
بس... القهوة كتبت حياتي على مزاجها !!

I drank the coffee the way I like it

But . . . the coffee . . wrote my fate the way it liked!![*]

[*]It is common practice in many Mediterranean cultures to predict the future by reading coffee grounds.

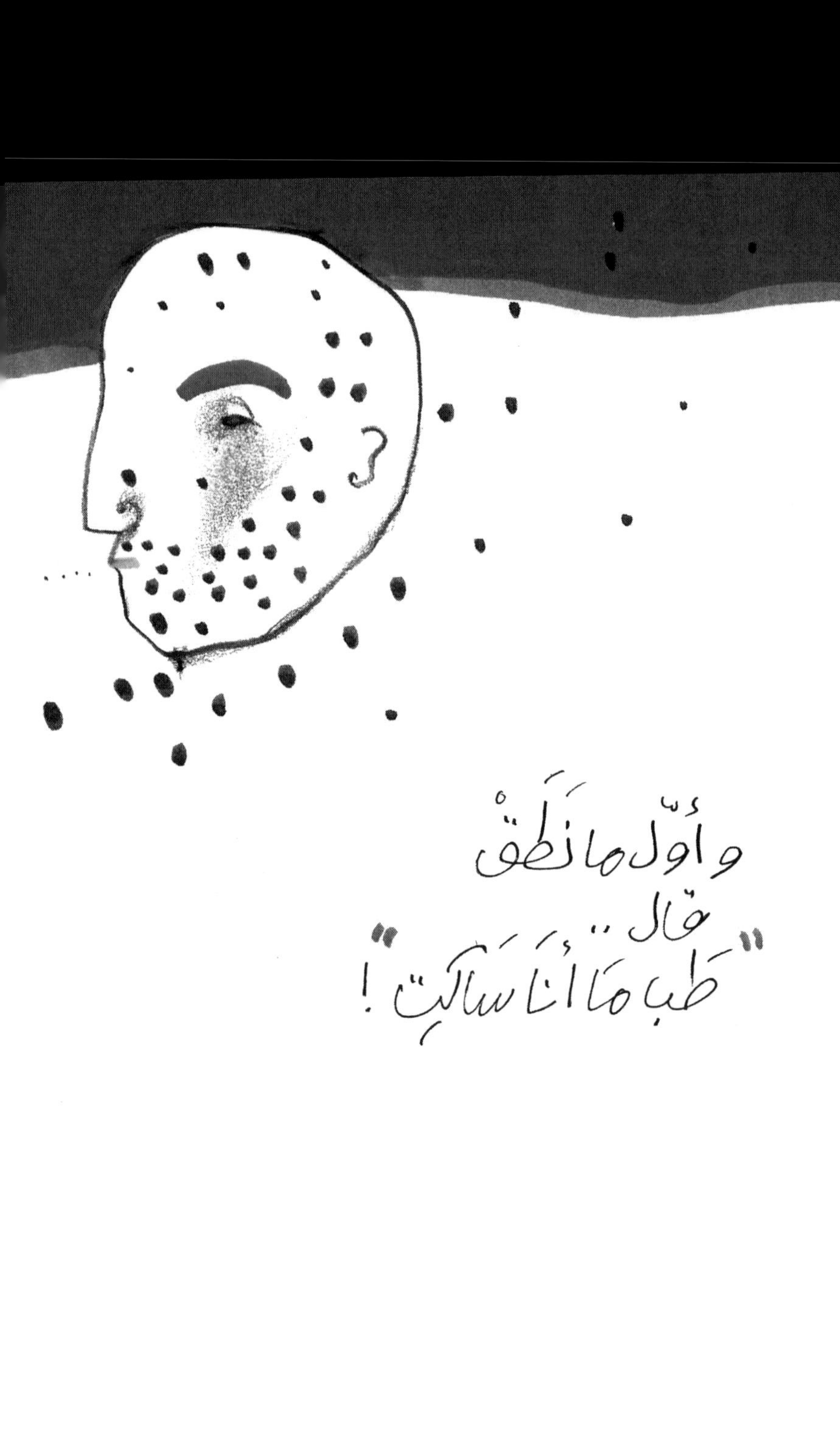
وأوّل ما نَطَقْ
قال..
"طَب ما أنا ساكِت"!

His first words

Were . .

"But I didn't say a word!"

طُول ما النّهار فارغ ...
اللّيل هَيِمْلاه !

As long as the day is empty . . .

The night will fill it!

حرقوا دَمّي
لِغاية
ما الفَتايِلّة وَلَّعِت !

They boiled my blood

Until

My undershirt caught on fire!

كان نِفْسي
أشوف نَفْسي
مِش خروف .....
.... قَبْل ما أنْدِبح !

I have always wished

I could see myself

As something other than a sheep . . . . .

. . . . before my slaughter!

الليّل هو الشّاي ...
و النهار هو اللبّن .
...... حُط ده على ده .. وإنتَ تدُوق طعم الزّمن !

The night is tea . . .

And the day is milk.

. . . . . . Mix them together . . and you will savor the taste of time!

.. هـا ... تشربى إيه ؟!
بس بُصى .. بلاش كاپوتشينو ...
ولا اللّى عليه .. وبلاش نسكافيه
وبلاش شاىّ أخْضر .. وبلاش شاى فَتْلة
وبلاش من ده .. ولا من ده ولا من ده
يا **نوال** .. أنا معاييش إلّا .. رُبْع جنيه !

So, what do you want to drink?!

But look here . . not cappuccino . . .

Not anything frothy . . not Nescafé

Not green tea . . nor fancy tea bags

None of this . . none of that

Oh, **Nawwal**, I only have . .

a quarter!

يا بخت الغُبار
والذرّات الصُغيّرة اللُذاذ
اللّي بترقص
وتلعب
وتدور ف النور
أدام الإزاز !

Oh you lucky dust

You sweet, small particles

That dance,

Play,

And twirl in the light

Outside my window!

بصّيت للقطّة ف عينها ....
....
القُطَط ...
عارفين حاجات .. إحْنا مِش عارفينها !

I looked the cat in the eye . . . .

. . . .

For cats . . .

Know things . . we don't know!

. لو سمحت الساعة كام ؟!

* الساعه دلوقتي تمام

. شكرا ... سلاموا عليكو ا

* عليكم السلام !

12

- Excuse me, what is the time?!
- The time is now
- Thank you . . . good-bye
- Good-bye!

في الأوضة
كانت المروحة زي الريح
وأنا زي.. النسر
واخدني الكلام والهبل..
فضلت أطير وأطير وأطير
لما فقت..
لقيت إن السرير
مش زي الجبل ...

In the room

The fan was my wind

And I . . the eagle

The dream and nonsense took me away

I kept flying, flying, flying

Only to wake . .

And find the bed

Was no mountain . . .

• أفكّر فى إيه؟
أفكّر فى إيه .. أفكّر فى إيه؟؟

* وإنت تفكّر ليه؟!

• أفكر ليه!..
أفكّر ليه .. أفكّر ليه؟!
أفكر ليه؟!

- What to think about?

  What to think about . . what to think about??

- Why do you think?!

- Why think!

  Why think . . why think?!

  Why think?!

إلبس أحمر
ووردي وبمبه
وكل الألوان الفاقعة
وإتحرك... وصرّخ
..يمكن يرد الدم
لاطرافك
الزرقا
الساقعة....!

Wear red,

Rose, magenta,

And all bold colors

And move . . . and shout

Perhaps the blood may revive

Your cold

Blue

Limbs . . . . !

يا بختك يا ابن الإيه ...

جبت الهبل ده كله منين ؟!

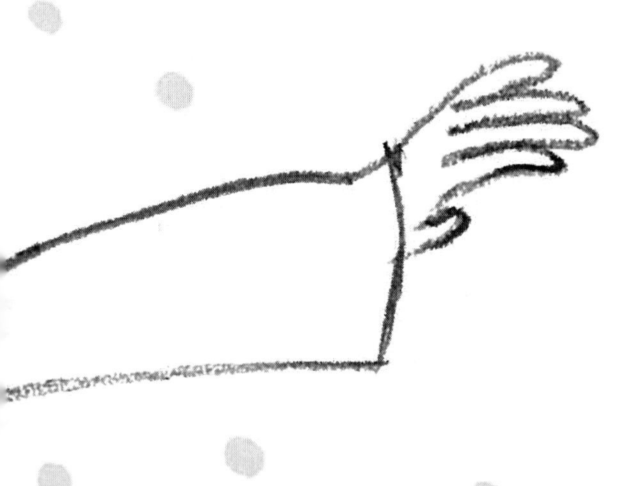

Oh you lucky bastard . . .

Where did you get all that foolishness?!

الشجر محطوط كده وكده
ف جنينة كده وكده..
قاعدين فيها ولد وبنت
بيقولوا لبعض
كلام...
كده وكده...!

The trees are laid out, willy-nilly

In the garden, willy-nilly . .

Where a boy and girl are sitting

Saying to each other

Words . . .

Willy-nilly . . !

ملك
سلطان
رئيس
مدير
ناظر
مش فارقة كتير
أهي كلها أسامي
وكلهم مناظر !!

King

Sultan

President

Manager

Principal

All the same

All just names

All for show!!

ليه العجلاتي قاعد كده ؟
وعنده كل العجل ده
أنا لو مِنّه
كل يوم أهرب
وماأرجعش !..

Why is the bike-renter just sitting there?

If I were him,

With all those bikes,

I would ride off every day

And not return!

بأجري
أجري
أجري
لقيت حيطة في وشي
دخلت فيها
وقعدت أجري
وأجري وأجري ..!

I run

Run

Run

Until I hit a wall

I go right through it

And again start to run

run, run . . !

أُدّام السور....
و أُدّام إللى بانيه....
و ادّام إللى بيْعَلّيه...
و ادّام إللى واقف يحميه
وقف راجل غلبان..
وعمل پيپيه!...

In front of the wall . . . .

In front of the one who built it . . . .

In front of the one who made it taller . . .

In front of the one who guards it

A poor guy stopped . .

And went pee pee! . . .

أَشْتَاقُ إلى الأَرْضِ التي
سأَصِلُ إليها
أشتاقُ إلى السَّماءِ التي
سَأَصْعَدُ إليها
أشتاقُ إلى البلكونة التي....
.... رموني منها...!

I long for the ground

Where I will be found

I long for the sky

To which I will fly

I long for the balcony . . . .

. . . . off which they threw me . . !

والنبي يا شتا

وحياة ولادك

البَرْد والشبّورة والضباب

بلاش المرّة دي لما تيجي

تيجي وتجيب لي

إكتئاب . . . . . . !

Swear, oh Winter,

By the lives of your children:

The cold, the mist, and the clouds

That this time when you come

You won't bring me

Depression . . . . . . !

كَتَبْتْ .. كَتَبْتْ .. كَتَبْتْ
هُسْ إتْكِتِمْ ... إتْكَتَمْتْ ...
كَبَتْ ..
إكْتَأَبْتْ
كَأَنِّي صُرْصَارْ
وإتْقَلَبْتْ !!

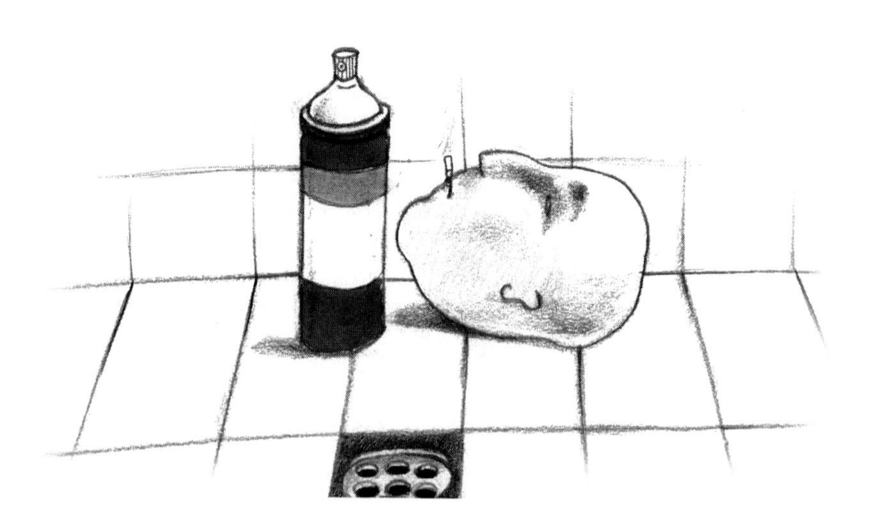

I wrote . . wrote . . . wrote

"Hush, shut up!"

I shut up . .

Thus suppressed

I got depressed

Like a cockroach

Flipped on its back!!

جريت استخبى من قَدَرى
لقيت المخبأ .... هُوَّ قَدَرى !!

I ran for shelter from my fate

Only to find that the shelter . . . . is my fate!!

بالحبر الإسود
إزّاى أقدر
أرسم
وردة روز !!

With black ink

How can I

Draw

A rose pink!!

أيوه.. بقيت إنسان
بس ليه حرموني من سجيتي
من دُنيتي...
ماليش دعوة..
أنا عاوز... حيوانيتي!

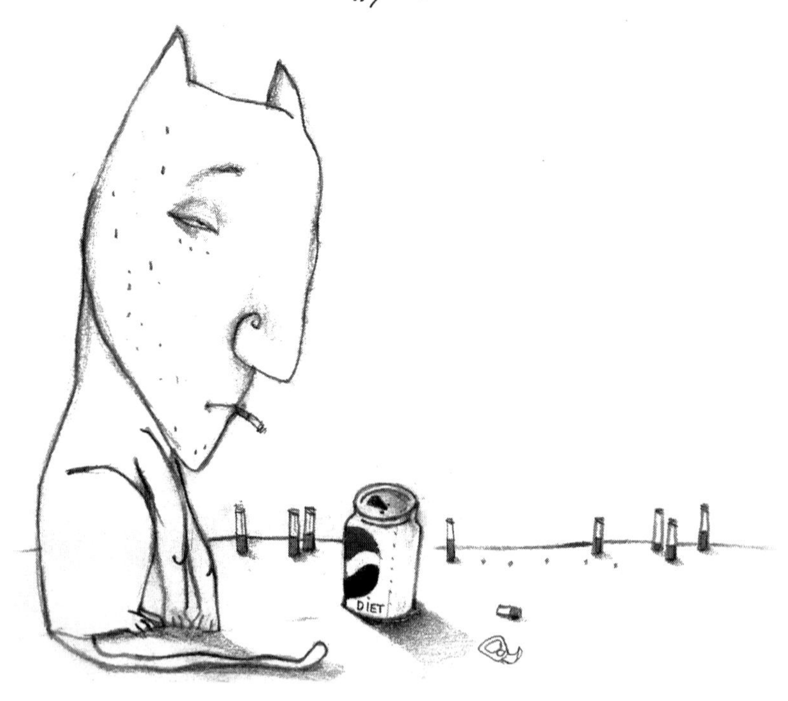

Yeah, so . . I've become human

But why did they take away my nature

My world . . .

I won't have any of this . .

Take me back . . . to the wild!

بتبُصّى كده ليه ؟!....

Why are you staring at me like that?! . . . .[*]

[*]Refrain from an old Egyptian folk song.

A donkey loved a dove . . .

She said, "But you're a donkey"

He said, "But a sensitive one

I write poetry and sing day and night

If you say yes, my love . . .

I will learn to fly . . and fix myself a beak

And become . . a dovely donkey

Not the ass I am!!"

حمار حبّ عصفورة ...
قالت له .. بس أنت حمار
قال لها .. بس رقيق
وبأكتب أشعار وبأغنّي ليل ونهار
لو وافقتي .. يا حبيبتي ....
هأتعلم الطيران .. وهأركّب منقار
وهأكون .. حمار عصفور
مش زي ما أنا ..
حمار ... حمار !!

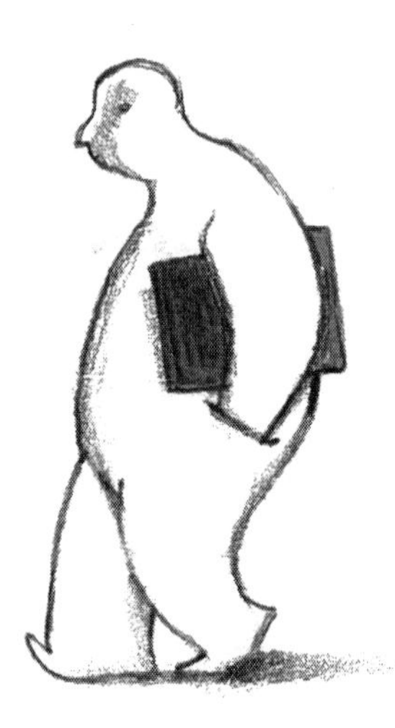

واحد عادى
ماشى هادى
روّح نام .. صحى
لقّى نفسه ....
واحد عادى !

An average Joe

Walking slow

Went home, slept . . woke

Only to find himself . . . .

an average Joe!

في كهف غويط...
تحت بحر بعيد...
فيه سمكة مستنّية...
أبُص في عينيها حبًّا
..وهي... تبُص حبًّا... في عينيّ!....

Tucked away in a cave . . .

Deep under the sea . . . .

A fish is waiting for me . . .

To gaze deep into her eyes

. . and for her . . . to gaze . . . deep into mine! . . . .

12

الساعة بتنخر في عضمي
وأنا عضمي قراقيش ....
تنخر .. تنخر .. تنخر
لحد ما هابقى .....
مافيش!

9 3

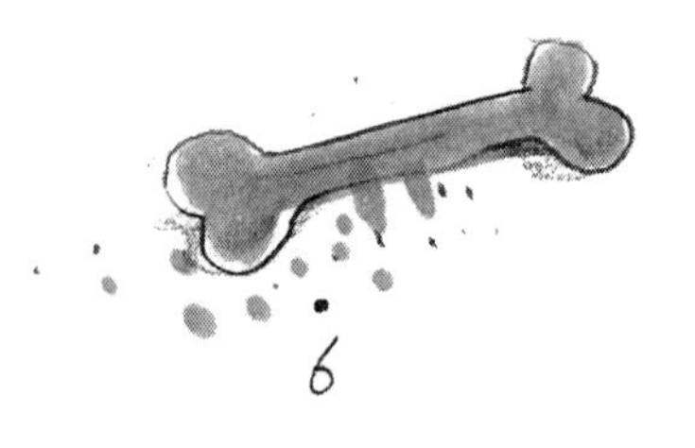

6

Time gnaws away at my bones

But my bones are already broken . . . .

Gnaw . . gnaw . . gnaw,

'Til I'm . . . . .

gone!

قال الحرامي النبيه
لأخيه ...

The sly thief told

His brother . . .

"Rather than cursing darkness

Steal under its cover!!"

- أنا مش هاقول حاجة لحد تاني...

- حاجة إيه؟

- أنا مش هاقول حاجة لحد تاني!...

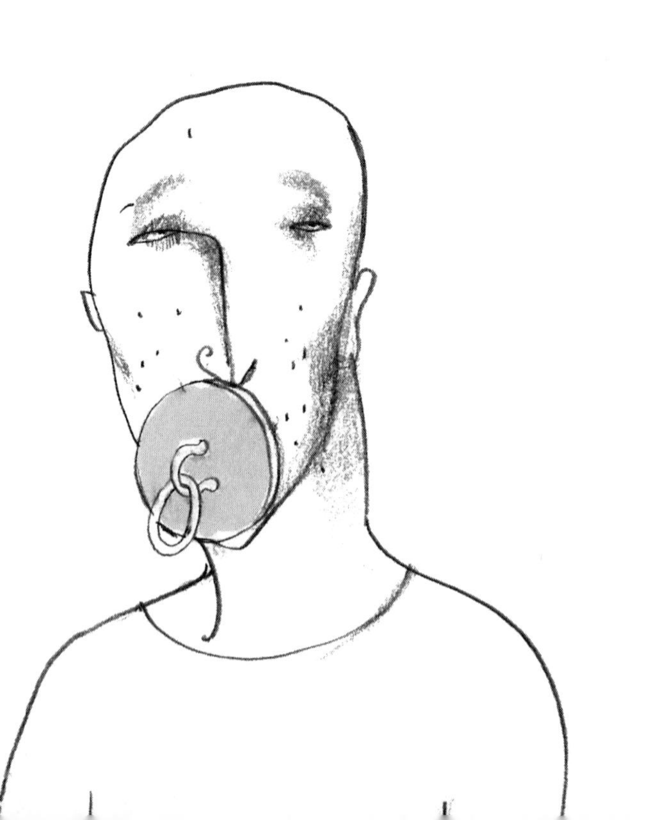

- I will never say anything
  To anyone else . . .

□ Say what?

- I will never say anything
  To anyone else! . . .

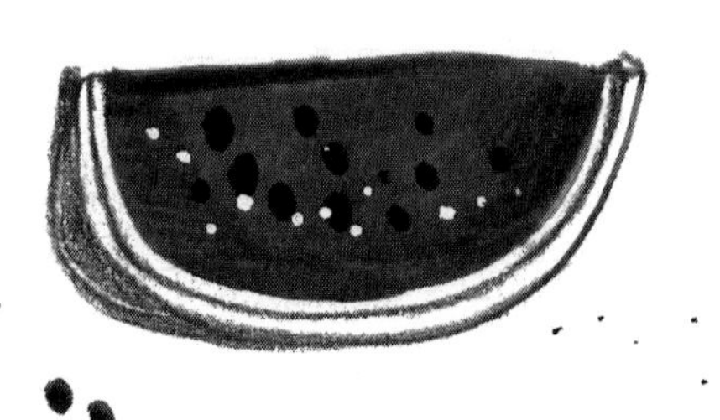

البطيخ كان أحمر صاحي
وبيضحك معانا
بقى ...
أزرق
ساكت !

When the watermelon was fresh and red

It used to laugh with us

Then it turned . . .

Blue

And silent!

آدينى أَهُه
و آدى قلبى . . .
و روحى وإيدى ومناخيرى
و عينى . . .
يلّلا بقى
يلّلا . . . .
حِبّينى !

Here I am

With my heart . . .

My soul, my hands, my nose

And my eyes . . .

Come on, already

Come on, and . . . .

Love me!

مات من الضحك
وفارق الحياة
مع إنها كانت نكتة
مش عاجباه !

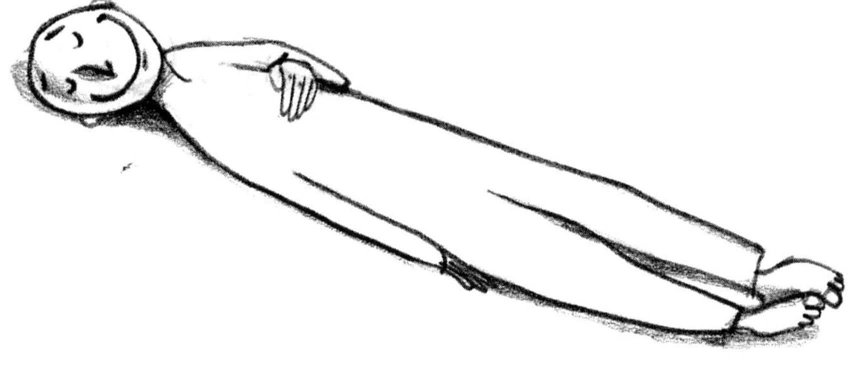

He died from laughing

And parted with life

Even though it was a joke

He didn't like!

لكْ حُبّي

وفقري وبهدلتي وأقساطي
وانحطاطي وإحباطي من مُرَتّبي
اللّي مِش كافي وذُلّي
ودلدلة كتافي
وعيني المكسورة أُدّام ولادي
من قُصْر الأيادي

وفؤادي!

To you I pledge my love

My poverty, my misery, and my debt

My failures and frustration with my meager salary

To you I pledge my humiliation,

My head hung low

And my eyes avoiding those of my children

For whom I can't provide

To you I pledge my heart![*]

[*]The first and last lines are from the Egyptian national anthem.

وزيّ ما احنا
زيّ ما صحينا
جرادل طحينة
واقعة على جرادل طحينة
كلنا واقعين
من بعض ....
على بعضينا!

Just as we slept

We woke

Buckets of tahini

Falling on buckets of tahini

All of us falling

From each other . . . .

onto each other!

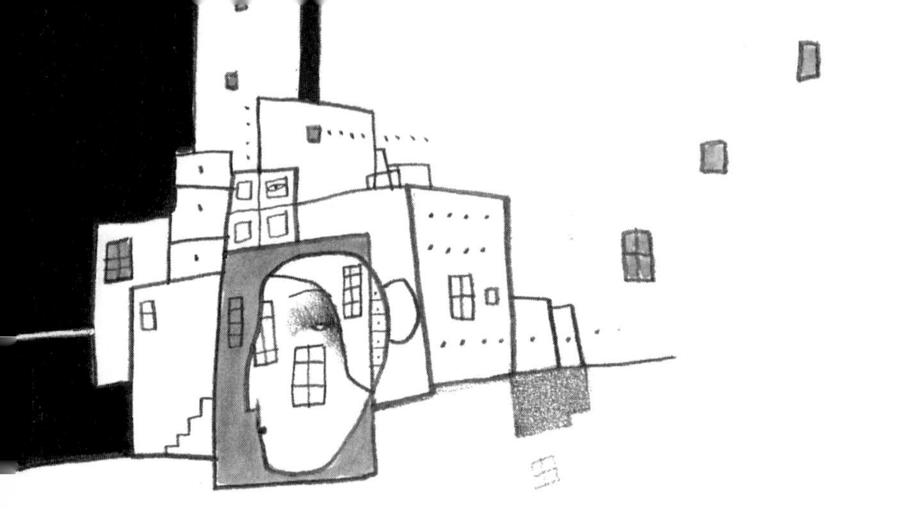

العُيُونْ بُيُوتْ

و البُيُوتْ أَسْرار ....!

Eyes are homes

And homes are secrets . . . . !

إمْبارح كُنت بأتكلّم مع نفسي

نمت .....

و لمّا صحيت ...

لقيت نفسي لسّه ماسكتّش ..!

Last night I was talking to myself

I slept . . . . .

And woke . . .

To find myself still talking away!

سلامتك يا مالك يا حزين
هيّ الطيور كده ..
دايمًا محسودين !

Feel better, kingfisher

You know how birds are . .

Always afflicted by the evil eye!

لا مش انا اللى أبكى
ولا أنا إللّى أحكى
ولا أنا إللّى أشكى
ولا حتى إللّى أتْفلق
أنا إللى بأضحك لغاية
مابتْخنق!

No, I'm not one to cry

I'm not one to sigh

I'm not one to pout

Or even pull my hair out

Instead, I am the one who laughs

Until I choke!*

*The first and third lines are taken from a famous folk song by Mohammed Abdel Wahab.

قعدت على تلات ترابيزات
وطلبت تلات طلبات
طلبت قهوة .... سكّر زيادة
ومُفتاح للسّعادة
وقلب حيّ بدل اللّى راح منّى
وانا فى منتهى البلادة!

I sat down at three tables

And ordered three things:

Coffee . . . . with extra sugar,

The key to happiness,

And a **beating** heart to replace the one I lost

when I was an utter fool!

هُعونه!!

Heartburn!!

وليد
٢٠٠٨

خمس ترغفة
محروقين
..واخدين
خمس ترغفة
محروقين !!

Five burnouts

. . Holding

Five burnt

Loaves!!

ما تبقاش حمار
وتحوّش الأفكار
وخلّيك قنبلة دايماً
ما تبطلش إنفجار ..!

Don't be an ass

Stockpiling your ideas

Be the bomb

That keeps going off . . !

Behind her husband's back, he snuck her a glance

Short and sweet . .

Behind her husband's back, she snuck him a glance

Short and sweet

Then she turned to her husband at the wheel and said . . . .

"Why don't you love me?!"

بَصّ لها من ورا جوزها

بَصّة حلوة ..

بصّت له من ورا جوزها

بَصّة حلوة

وقالت لجوزها اللّى سايق ....

"إنت ليه مش بتحبّنى"؟!

إمبارح وأنا مروّح
ما دخلتش في شارعنا... ودخلت في شارع تاني
تُهت.. بس شفت...
شجر تاني...
باب تاني...
كلب تاني...
بكره وأنا مروّح
مش هاروّح
وهاسيب نفسي
أتوه تاني!.

Yesterday on my way home

I missed our street . . . and turned on a different one

Lost . . I saw . . .

Different trees . . .

A different door . . .

A different dog . . .

Tomorrow on my way home

I won't go home

I'll let myself

Get lost again!

إيه قيمة إنَّك حصان جميل ...
بس مَرْبُوط ....
أو نِسْر عظيم مُحنَّط .. مَحطوط
لا يا عم .. خلّيني زي ما أنا
قرد مجهول ....
بس مَبْسوط !

What's the use in being a beautiful horse . . .

But tied up . . . .

Or a great eagle, mummified . . set aside

No, sir, leave me as I am

An unnoticed monkey . . . .

But happy!

..والغسّاله و... التليفون والتليفزيون والشّاحن

.. والسلّم والستارة والمرايه والكنبة و... السّاعة و...

وأهرب..

أنا والبلكونة!

مسيري أصحى ف يوم
وأقتل التلاجه والبوتوجاز والسخان...
والشفاط والمكوه واللمبة والحيطان و..

I'm bound to wake up one day

And shoot the fridge, stove, and heater . . .

The fan, iron, lamp, and walls . .

. . the washer, TV, phone and charger,

. . the stairs, curtains, mirror, sofa, and clock . . .

And run away . .

With the balcony!

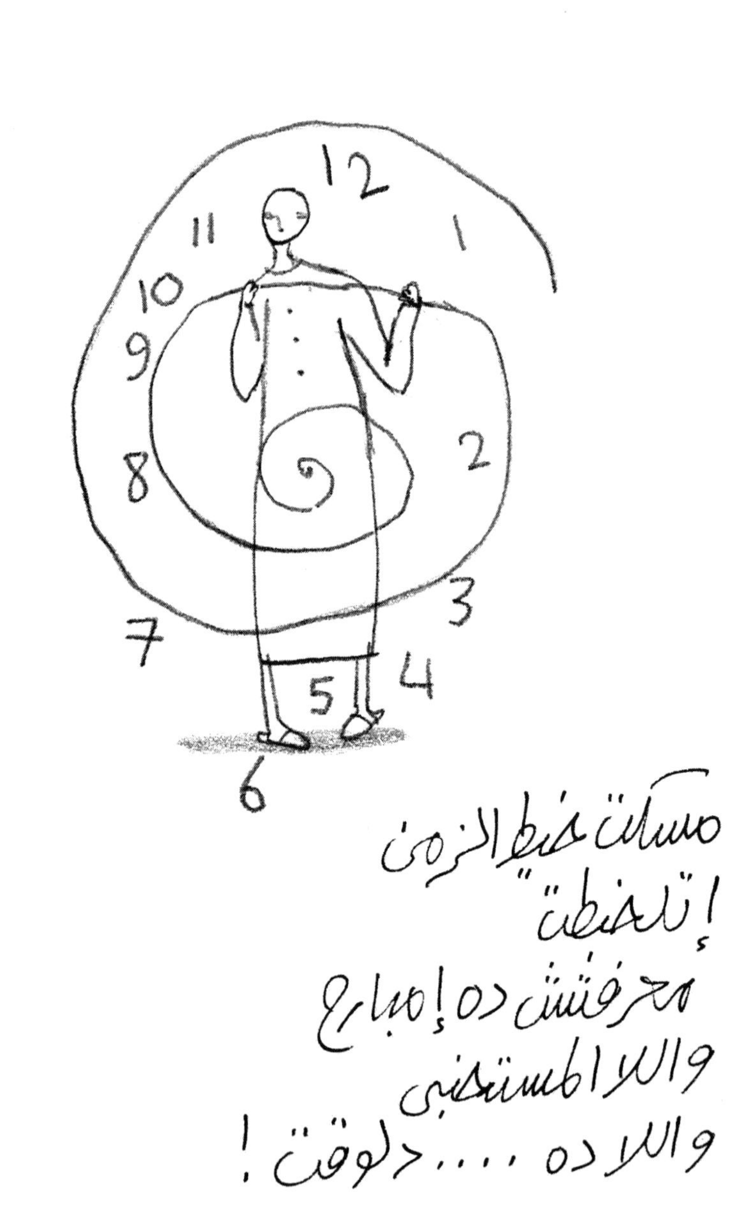

مسكت خيط الزمن
إتلخبطت
معرفتش ده إمبارح
والا المستقبل
والا ده .... دلوقت!

I held the thread of time

And got confused

I couldn't tell if it was yesterday

Or what may come

Or . . . . now!

كابوس شتوي !!

فيل أعمى عجوز
بيجري على ضهره
ألف نملة فارسي
هرش..
هربوا كلهم.. ما اتبقاش منهم
إلا نملة.. قرصتني
صحتني
لمحتها...
قتلتها.. وبعدها
حسّيت
بإكتئاب الفش !!

A chilling nightmare!!

A thousand fire ants

Running on the back

Of a blind old elephant

He scratched . .

They all ran away . . all of them

Except one . . it bit me

And woke me up

I caught a glimpse of it . . .

Killed it . . and afterwards

I felt

Winter blues!!